This Book Belongs To:

----

age: _____

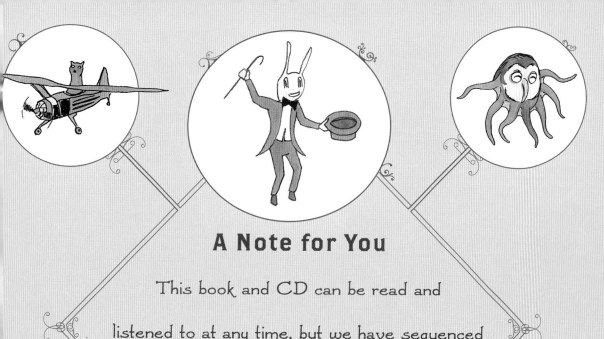

A Note for You

This book and CD can be read and

listened to at any time, but we have sequenced

the stories to help parents and kids

find their way to

slumberland.

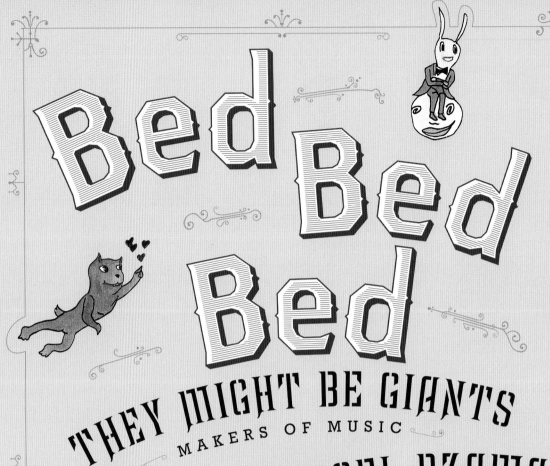

Bed Bed Bed

THEY MIGHT BE GIANTS
MAKERS OF MUSIC

AND

Illustrated by MARCEL DZAMA
MASTER ARTIST

SIMON & SCHUSTER
NEW YORK LONDON TORONTO BROOKLYN
SYDNEY WINNIPEG SINGAPORE

This book
is dedicated to
Henry

THANKS TO
GEOFF,
SAM,
PAT,
KAREN,
& ROBIN

Simon & Schuster
Rockefeller Center
1230 Avenue of the Americas
New York, NY 10020

Library of Congress
Cataloging-in-Publication data
is available.

ISBN 0-7432-5024-9

For information regarding special discounts for bulk purchases,
please contact Simon & Schuster Special Sales at
1-800-456-6798 or business@simonandschuster.com

1 3 5 7 9 10 8 6 4 2

DESIGNED BY SAM POTTS INC.

MANUFACTURED IN CHINA

IMPOSSIBLE

Well, they said I was impossible.

Yes, they said I was impossible

and that someone who behaved like me

couldn't be, couldn't be.

But I knew that I was possible,

not completely unbelievable,

and the one they said could never be,

it was me, it was me.

But there's something else they didn't know:
You can change your shape and you can grow

out of nothing into something new,

something made up into something true,

though it happens quite impossibly,

the impossible turns out to be

possibly.

doh-doh doh-doh
doh-doh doh-doh

Well, I'd like to be an octofish.

Yes, I'd like to be an octofish.

That's the thing that I would like to be:

octofoo, octofee.

But they tell me it's impossible.

Yes, they say it is impossible.

It's a thing that I can never be,

never be, never be.

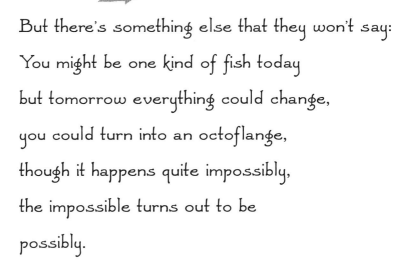

But there's something else that they won't say:

You might be one kind of fish today

but tomorrow everything could change,

you could turn into an octoflange,

though it happens quite impossibly,

the impossible turns out to be

possibly.

If you wish you had violet hair

that flows from your room down the stair,

if you want to run as fast as a car

or just want to be more like you are,

though it happens quite impossibly,

the impossible turns out to be

possibly.

doh-doh doh-doh
doh-doh doh-doh

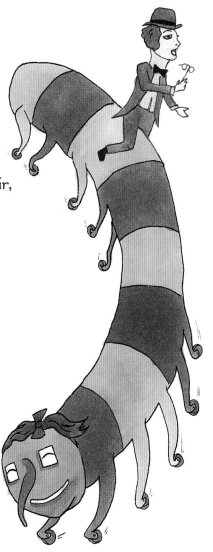

Happy

DOESN'T HAVE

HAVE

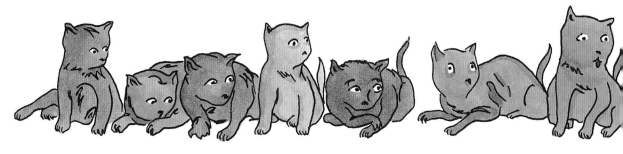

TO HAVE an Ending

Hip hip hippy hippy me today, Happy hippy hippy me today,
Hip hip hippy hippy me today, Happy hippy hippy me today.

I'm a long-haired hippie kitten.

I'm on a secret mission.

I've got a message for the people of the world:

You've got to know Happy doesn't have to have an ending!

Don't stop the good times when they start!

Come on now!

You've got to know Happy doesn't have to have an ending!

Remember this before we part:

You've got to sing out loud when the music starts.

You've got to shake your tail when you hear this part.

Come on now!

I'm a long-haired hippie kitten.
I'm on a secret mission
to make a valentine for everyone on earth.
I'm sitting in my window with my kitten arms akimbo.
My paw is tired from this valentines' work.

Gavotte's a kind of dance and
it really comes from France and
it's like a minuet but moderately fast.
Other cats come around here just to
gavotte with me and you too.
Put to rest the rumors that a hippie cat can't dance!

You've got to know Happy doesn't have to have an ending!

You've got to make room for too much fun.

Come on now!

You've got to know Happy doesn't have to have an ending!

We've got the stars.

We've got the sun.

You've got to smile awhile when it feels all right.

You've got to jump around, and we'll dance all night!

Come on now!

Hip hip hippy hippy me today, Happy hippy hippy me today,
Boom! I'm coming out of my room.
Hip hip hippy hippy me today, Happy hippy hippy me today,
Boom! I'm coming out of my room.
Hip hip hippy hippy me today, Happy hippy hippy me today.
Got a delivery for Mr. Peter Tork.
Got a valentine for Mr. Peter Tork.
Hip hip hippy hippy me today, Happy hippy hippy me today.

IDLEWILD

Sun shines bright on a hot summer day.

Roller coasters await.

See the sideshow at Steeplechase Park—

Test your strength, guess your weight.

Take a ride on a skywriting plane.

Loopty-loop for a while.

La la la La la la
La la la La la la

When we're done writing words in the sky

We'll land in Idlewild,

Idlewild,

Idlewild,

Idlewild,

Idlewild.

BED, BED, BED, BED, BED

SONG No. 4

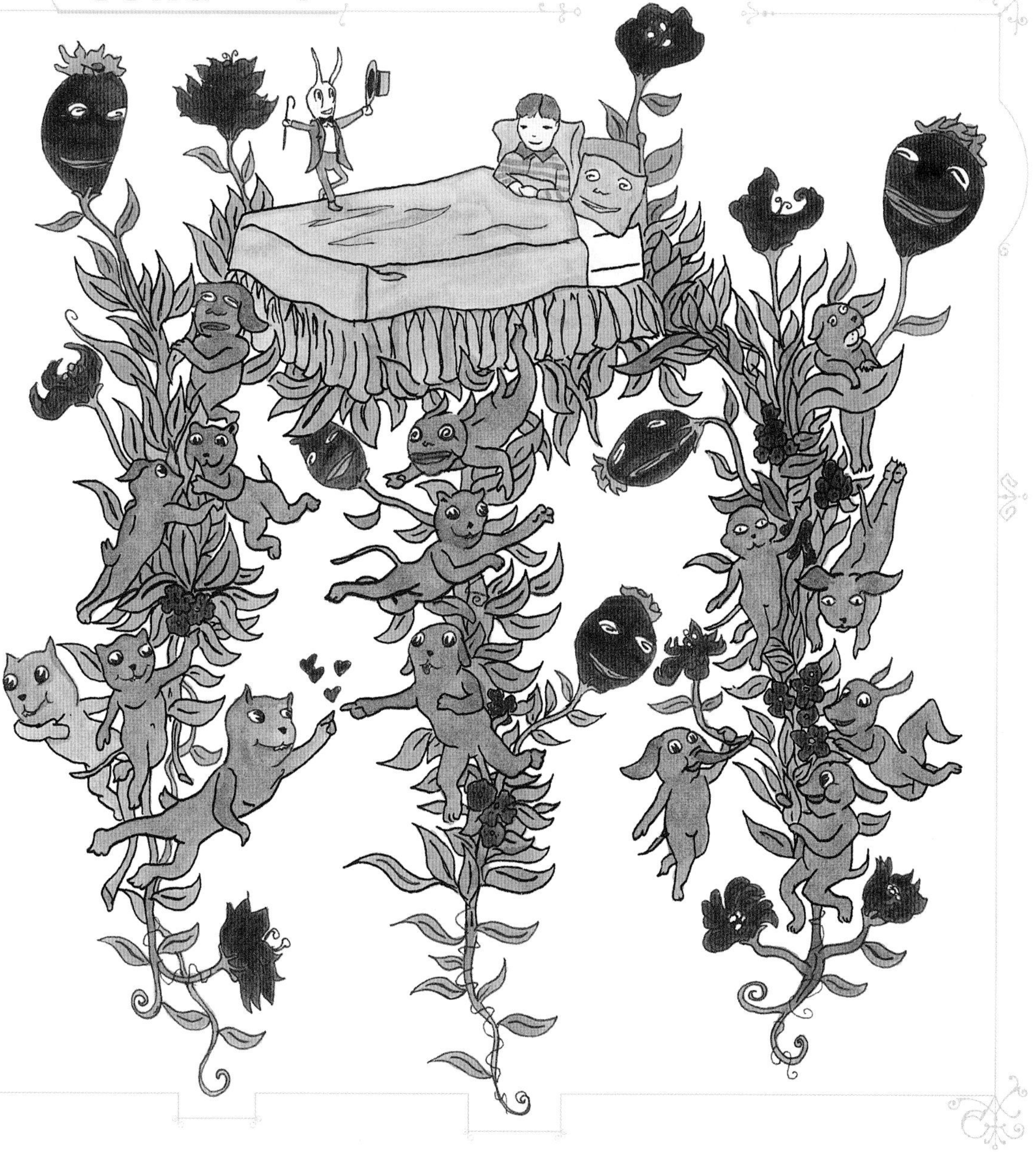

The day is done.

The sun is down.

The curtains have been drawn,

and darkness has descended over everything in town.

The covers have been turned,

and I've got my pajamas on.

I've had my fun.

I've stretched and yawned,

and all is said and done.

I'm going to bed!

Bed, bed, bed, bed, bed.

I've done so many things today
there's nothing left to do.

I ate three meals,

I rode my bike,

I hung out with my friends,

I did my chores,

I watched TV,

I practiced the guitar,

I brushed my teeth,

I read my book,

and then I sat around.

I'm going to bed!

Bed, bed, bed, bed, bed.

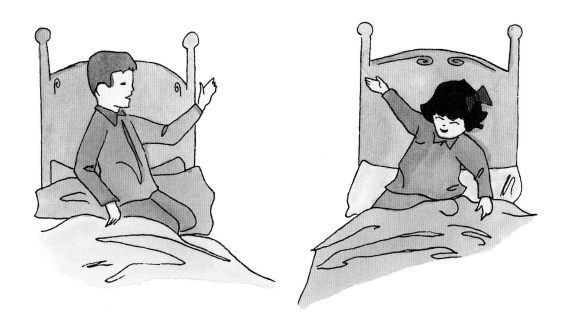

Oh, it's pointless staying up for even twenty seconds more

when everything has happened

and there's nothing else in store.

The thing is now to lay my head down,

close my eyes, and snore.

And so to bed directly I go.

And so to bed directly I go.

The day is done.

The sun is down.

The curtains have been drawn,

and darkness has descended over everything in town.

The covers have been turned, and I've got my pajamas on.

I've had my fun.

I've stretched and yawned,

and all is said and done.

I'm going to bed!

Bed, bed, bed, bed, bed.

I'm going to bed!

Bed, bed, bed, bed, bed.

THE END

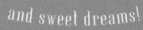
Good night . . .
and sweet dreams!